World over Water

World over Water

poems by
ROBERT GIBB

THE UNIVERSITY OF ARKANSAS PRESS

Fayetteville

2007

11   10   09   08   07   5   4   3   2   1

Text design by Ellen Beeler

♾ The paper used in this publication meets the minimum requirements of
the American National Standard for Permanence of Paper for Printed
Library Materials z39.48-1984.

Library of Congress Cataloging-in-Publication Data

Gibb, Robert.
World over water : poems / by Robert Gibb.
    p. cm.
  ISBN-13: 978-1-55728-836-3 (pbk. : alk. paper)
  ISBN-10: 1-55728-836-4 (pbk. : alk. paper)
  I. Title.
  PS3557.I139W67 2007
  811'.54—dc22

                                        2006034204

for Maggie,
for Matthew & Andrew

"The past is here." He touched his heart.

—Naipaul, *A Bend in the River*

ACKNOWLEDGMENTS

"Touring Clayton, the Estate of the Industrialist Henry Clay Frick" and "*Trapper Boy, Coal Mine,*" *Chelsea;* "The Hall of Architecture," *The Georgia Review;* "On the Photographs in Margaret Byington's *Homestead: The Households of a Mill Town*" and "Park Elementary School," *The Hudson Review;* "Raising the Blinds" and "*Pittsburghesque, Ca. 1949,*" *The Kenyon Review;* "Hettie," *The Laurel Review;* "Lewis Hine in Homestead," *Margie;* "Smokestack Lightning," *Meridian;* "Deed," "At the History Center, Remembering a Photograph Taken of My Father," and "At the Steelworkers' Monument During the 100th Anniversary of the Homestead Strike of 1892," *The Missouri Review;* "Industrial Relics, Station Square," *Notre Dame Review;* "The Bandstand," *Pittsburgh Post-Gazette;* "Industrial Landscapes," *Ploughshares;* "Saying Farewell to the Displays in the Museum of Natural History" and "Wood Frog, Frick Park," *Poetry;* "Steelworkers' Lockers, Pittsburgh History Center" (as "Relics") and "Fingered" (as "Enough"), *Poetry East;* "Water Music," "*Alexander Berkman Addressing May First Rally, Union Square, New York, 1908,*" "Berkman in Prison: Woods Run, 1900," "The Homestead Lockout & Strike, 1892," "Melville Views the Homestead Works," and "Khrushchev Visits Mesta Machine, 1959: A Variation on the Double Sonnet," *Prairie Schooner;* "Charting the Leaves," *Shenandoah;* "Nocturne," "328 Sixteenth Avenue," "Class Photos," "The Art of the Comics, Ca. 1960," "At Kennywood Park," "Gallery Guide," and "*Dream Street:* W. Eugene Smith's Pittsburgh Photo-graphs," *The Southern Review;* "Wood Work," *Tar River Poetry;* "Aftermath" and "*Mesta Worker and Gear, 1913,*" *West Branch.* Class Photos" and "Melville Views the Homestead Works," respectively, were reprinted in *Poetry Calendar 2006* and *Poetry Calendar 2007,* edited by Shafiq Naz, Alhambra Publishing.

Acknowledgement is also due to the Pennsylvania Council on the Arts, a grant from which was crucial in the completion of this manuscript.

CONTENTS

World over Water

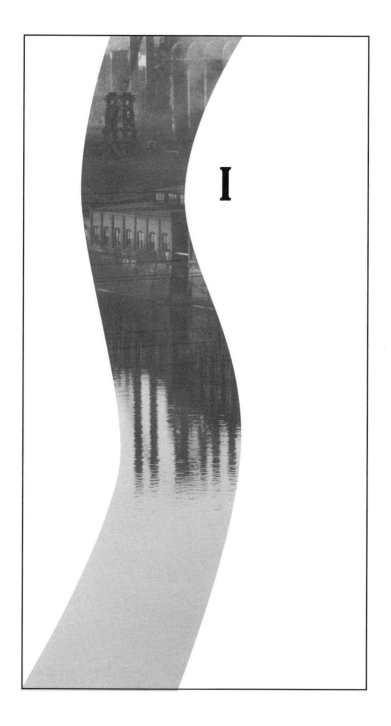

I

INDUSTRIAL LANDSCAPES

A.H. Gorson, 1872–1933

"The Pittsburgh school," his colleagues called
This vision of the city, massed shapes laid
Against the light that showered up, impasto,
From their midst—river and mill yard and wharf—
The forms he dissolved or cast into relief
Or drew more massive in the general noon.
Unlike the other tonal painters, he worked upward
From the stain, freighting his brush with paint.

In *Pittsburgh at Night,* for instance, white smoke
And the acetylene flash of metals being tapped,
The Bessemer conversion of cast iron into steel,
Are arrayed against the beryl of river and sky,
The silhouetted colonnades of the chimneys.
I stood before those familiar waters for hours,
Growing up, at the picture plane of the foreground
On which the cropped, dark barges still float.

I think I liked it because it seemed a facet
Of the landscape I'd pass through coming home,
Vantages in the distance held in similar scale.
But really it was a world Gorson had made his own,
Though soot from the stacks soiled his canvases
And he worked on the paintings in a studio
Whose windows blazed at night: undraped citron
In a city gone to monochrome all around him.

If he'd lived here later he could have sketched
The erasures of light in which the great sheds
Were dismantled—brownfield sites he'd wash
With the stain of oxides. Perched on the bridge
As in the sky, he could plot out lines of perspective,
Bird's eye and horizon, the vanishing points
From which the skeleton girders streamed apart.
Back in his rooms, he could grid them in again.

SAYING FAREWELL TO THE DISPLAYS IN THE MUSEUM OF NATURAL HISTORY

Dakota, Arapaho, Laguna Pueblo . . .
The nations displayed in booths in their dim,
Third-story rooms where mannequins were
Grouped in poses: women gathering patterns
At their looms, warriors in robes, priests
In mid-rapture amid the slack, lulled beadwork
Of the snakes. Here, where time was geologic,
I'd find them at the same pursuits as always,
As if shaped by an enormous patience.

They made you invisible. Like the museum's
Other plunder, they taught how seeing
Was a way of inhabiting time. I know,
They were clichés, fixed in nineteenth-century
Niches, stolid as though carved from wood.
They were like the movies, all wrong
Even when rightly arrayed with breechcloths
And moccasins, the frescoed vistas against
Which they were set. And yet they were also

An amplitude in the world I knew of swing shifts
And row homes, smoke in pillars above the mills.
I owed them a last farewell, but the room
Was already closed. Through a rip in the tarp,
I could see work tables and coils of rope among

The half-dismantled booths, a figure I'd known
Since childhood stripped naked on the floor,
Chipped leg dropped before it, like the bodies
At Pine Ridge, only so much more wreckage.

DEED

for the purpose of human sepulcher alone

Crosswise from the plaque for the Homestead martyrs
And back down the slope past the Protestant edge of things,

I have come to stand here once again, importuning my dead.
ROBERT GIBB, the stone says, three chiseled links

Of a chain above the blocked-out letters. And the dates,
1870–1905, since this is the grave of my father's father,

The machinist who died in the mills. In the photos of him
That survive—stiff, mounted, sepia prints—

He stands posed beside the enormous shears and presses
He worked upon, his arm cocked on the lever

Of the industrial world. A world that's now faded as well,
The color of the dust into which my father's ashes

Have been scattered in turn, as though he'd been flung
Back into the stone and a name that was also his own.

Been flung as well into the rusted limbs of the pitch pine
Twisting above him, the burning patches of grass

The color of the deed I hold to the other half of this plot.
A hundred years ago my grandfather bought it,

Having buried one wife already and providing for the next,
For *his heirs and assigns, forever.* He only had one—

The sintered son who's entered the ground around him,
A trace of metals returning to the earth—

Who himself had only the one, who now stands within
The *120 superficial feet* of all here that he owns,

All that's been left but the name given three times in a row
To an heir half-orphaned in infancy. A name like a birthmark

Or bruise in the blood, congenital for generations,
And a rock of stone in which the name might finally repose.

The name on the deed is the color of rust,
Which is blood and metal.

STEELWORKERS' LOCKERS,
PITTSBURGH HISTORY CENTER

The Forlornness of Metal they might as well
Be titled, these salvaged relics, props from a set
Long struck—the lap-welds and louvers
And green latch-locked doors bolted in line
In assembly, each the width of a man crammed in
Or hung in parts as in effigy. The bench hard
As a pew. Beyond, the mills were medieval,
Rows of stoves set four to the furnace, chimneys
In groves, hoists where they elevated the stock.

In the locker room, at the start of each shift,
Shucked aluminum suits got lowered on pulleys
From their ceiling roosts. We changed into
Forge-proof shoes, the hardhat's Day-Glo halo,
And stepped among flames, out into the annealing,
Where the world was turned to steel.

AT THE HISTORY CENTER, REMEMBERING
A PHOTOGRAPH TAKEN OF MY FATHER

1.

The dust raised up! Brick and girders remitted
From the slow fires of the rust, the gray
Particulate Pittsburgh air that fell upon us
Like history's patina and surface glare.
Here all's restored: the U.S. Steel insignia,
Klein's neon lobster and scalloped seas—
The sign beneath which my parents dined
During their brief spring following the war,
Before her death left him shell-shocked.

2.

I climb into the softy glowing streetcar,
Mint and empty, they might have ridden.
The house in Homestead they returned to,
Past twisty rivers and smoke-plumed flues,
Looked just like this restoration with its
Weathered trim and kitchen, the mills' red
Suffusion flooding the shadowbox rooms.
Alleys I watched, in turn, fill with sparrows
And children flocking home from school.

3.

Outside there, just below the window,
The boy who became my father stands posed,
Archival in his baseball suit: hightops
And stirrups, the splayed glove dangling

To his knee like an enormous swollen paw.
In the glass above him the oil-rubbed fronds
And bird cage swirl within the white scrim
Of sunlight reflecting off the panes,
A framed world flattened like history.

4.

COAL his shirt reads, which the stove
In the kitchen burns, and the winter furnace,
As though time were sifting its cold iron grates
For the boy dressed so lovingly for play,
The snows he'll find each year pitted more
With ashes. Strung outside the window here,
Across the courtyard to the porch next door,
Worn clouds of laundry fill their line
With bodies more abiding than our own.

RAISING THE BLINDS

All day, by the window, I've been looking
To fathom such intricacies as these:
Hail, sleet, freezing rain, the heavy
Welter of flakes, and how each
Complements the other which seemed
At first a blur of the same emotion—
Misery or grief—some little alley
With its trash cans and garages, rutted
Snow, the brownout of the lamps.

And those figures down there, hurrying
Home or from it, lost beneath their
Umbrellas' tautened cloth, how the puddles
Each passes gleam like scraps of sky.
Cold yesterday and rain glazed
Every surface, cocooning the branches,
Slicking down the damp rooftop slates.
By the time it stopped I was already
Asleep. I was fast in my own waters.

Wasn't it Alfred Stieglitz who sought
To frame within his view-finder
Those equivalents of inner weather,
The clouds he'd dredge from the waters
Of the developer's vat? Dark, penumbral,
Or riddled with such light as filled them

Only for a time. Or, like today,
A gray relentless drizzle, as though
The private life went on without end.

2.

How it came in bags like hockey mitts,
Solid blocks of light
The color of breath on our windows,
Or steam rising from the manhole's chinks.

*

How it would be evening, as always,
The light like winter,
And my father still wearing his raincoat,
Clumps of dry ice clattering into the sink.

*

How they boiled there in the water,
Or stuck cold as metal
To the touch, smooth shards of tarnish,
Fog burning off the thaw like smoke.

3.

Winters, our windows wept
Wherever my stepmother sat:

Cold braids whose flow slowly
Wedged the casement locks open,

Spilling in thin frozen streams
Clear to the marble sills

Where they fused together,
Ropy and gray, frost etching

Its thick way across the panes.
At the sad end of the tables

Those seams kept seeping,
Prying the steel frames apart.

They looked like the quartz
That veined my favorite rock.

When finally she doused them
With boiling water, I watched

Ice wilt into a spill-off,
And never once thought to wonder

Why the world at her windows
Seemed so filled with sorrow

It kept groping into our rooms,
Rousing her to scald it

And fall at the locks once more,
Straining to snap them shut.

4.

Idle and April, the first storm of blossoms
Filling the trees, I stood watching my father
Plant his ladder in the crushed grade of gravel
Covering our drive, then test his weight

On the swayed stalks, climbing slowly above
The cinder blocks to the brick-line of the house.
And there he stood, out in the air beyond
His bedroom window, scaring birds away.

From up the street I could hear the familiar
Blades of mowers whirring across their lawns,
The voices from a ballgame on the radio.
Overhead, a contrail was being steadily erased.

Leaning against the bottom rungs, I watched
As weekend traffic eddied past, the birds
Resettled on their wires, evenly as time.
When the ladder shook me from my reverie,

I looked up to find my father struggling
With the storm window he was taking off—
A pane of light which lifted from the house
And crashed down all about me, like blossoms

In a gust. My skin glistening with slivers,
The sluice of my blood, the day went blank
About me there, at the foot of the ladder,
In the suddenly piercing air.

5.

One of love's small labors,
This leveling of the light
Into even wales, like lines
Ruled on paper. The blinds,
Valanced and drawn, take on
The look of an egg shell,
Our rooms lit as if candled
And arrayed before the world
Onto which they'll now open,
Scored for the various music
That fills them at the crack
Of the staff.

            The way again
This morning light breaks
Over Wilkinsburg and then
The whole westerly stretch
Of our street, to where
It ends in the teal and salmon
Trim on the two Victorians,
The last groups of children
Being packed off to school,
Their small hoards storming
The sidewalks.

            Then only
The sparrows returning
To their squabbles, the buses
Surging into their surfs
Where the rainy hum of traffic

Drowns Braddock Avenue,
Only the neighborhood dogs
Barking, a delivery truck
Rumbling past, sirens,
The clattering rush of blinds
Being raised behind the sash.

THE HALL OF ARCHITECTURE

There in the past's attic, we stopped before
Plinths and entablatures, caryatids
Topped with their vast crowns, a pair of cupids
Bearing small stone wings: all of it hoarded
In that hall whose remnants we ranged among,
Dwarfed by portals and urns, the castings
Of the great doors of a baptistry
Where every panel disgorged its throng.
Even the radiators seemed monumental.
You found such maleness smothering, marble
And bronze being brunted by the will.
I remembered the mills when molten steel
Poured into molds, slag rose like coral reefs,
The scale of that labor now hard to conceive.

But then this was my house of wonders
While growing up—the horse of the sun
Surging from its stone, the horse of the moon
Setting—the great room's freight and plunder
As natural to me as the cliff wall
Rising along West Run Road, dates and names
Scrawled across its rocks. It was all the same:
The lettered bluff, the museum's sheer vaults
Carded from their quarry. This was Pittsburgh,
After all. I rode home on welded tracks,
Past open hearths and dark, purling rivers,

Buildings constructed out of granite blocks.
For me the past was an escarpment—
Something silent and shelfed and permanent.

NOCTURNE

Pittsburgh winter: iron and old snow,
Buildings quarried from granite
   And gray nineteenth-century stone
      Fading in the dusk and mill smoke,

A few cars emptying from the lots,
Their parking lights burning. It must be
   Saturday since I am in Oakland, out
      Wandering the streets alone, having

Drawn for hours in the dim rooms
Of the museum, or looked at paintings
   I'd come to know as well as the ones
      In my childhood books. I know those

Bronze cats too, crouched at the corners
Of the Panther Hollow Bridge, the bare
   Trees of the park, but why I'm there,
      Headed away from the trolley home,

I don't remember, or why I've stopped
To stare down over the railing
   And find the pond filled with skaters
      Slowly orbiting the floor of the sky.

WATER MUSIC

Moored to its landing like a burning wharf,
　　The symphony barge floated on the Allegheny,

Lights already molten in the poured brass horns,
　　The starch-white coats of musicians

Who sat tethered there, warming into F major.
　　Twilight the texture of water spread around us,

And that hush from which the first bright bursts
　　Of Handel would emerge, quickening the air

Of Pittsburgh with strains from the Baroque.
　　Even then the music swirled like swallows,

Brisk notes circling upward to trace their flight
　　Through grains of sunlight giving way.

Forget for a moment that he composed it to celebrate
　　The British throne's victory at Culloden.

Forget the privileges of empire, the concrete ledge
　　Where you sat pressed against a wall

Of listeners glistening with the heat. Remember,
　　This once, the music: how each strain

Joined the others, the roiling of notes
        Like blue bodies and russet throats, tails precise

As tuning forks. You watched the circuits of water
        Take the air and wheel rounds there

In an intricate delight, and in spite of everything
        Have carried such headlong dancing with you

Across the years, and have managed such a vision
        Of the whole sky turned to song.

AFTERMATH

Driving past them again today—
Rubble and the open hearths'
Great rusted husks, boilers looming
Above the detonated acres—

I thought, as always, of Egypt,
Locusts as sallow as blighted crops,
And corn, those years of famine,
Long vanished from their stores.

That this is what it means
To live in history, as though
The past were a difficult music
To keep from your head.

Yesterday, driving home at twilight
Across the McKeesport Bridge,
I looked upriver: barge lights
And the white plume of smoke

From a remnant mill, water
The same blue nocturne as the sky's
Floating opaquely in place,
And everything else from the banks

To the crimps in the ridge-tops
A black so deep it seemed flocked.

It could have been years ago,
The great fires filling the valley,

Ingots being broken into blooms.
No ruins. No rust growing rankly
As flakes of fungus
Over metals peeling off in leaves.

I wonder, would I suffer the river
To bring it back, even though
I hated my days in the mills?
Last night, watching arc lamps

Burning softly above the water
Like the first evening stars,
The answer would have been *yes*.
Yes again this morning, seeing

The world in the welter of light,
The wards of McKeesport bleached
And laid bare as jetsam
Left rotting along that shore.

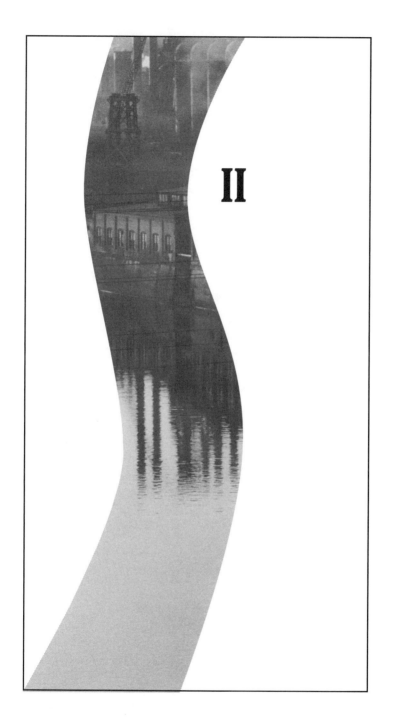

II

328 SIXTEENTH AVENUE

Backyard and alley, the buckled brick-weave of the walk.
It's 1948 and my softly lit face is filled with shadows
Like airbrushed clouds: a dark which in the photographs

Never matches the luster of my grandmother's patent boots,
Or the black flame of the locust flickering into leaf behind us
Against an opaque white sky. In what would have been

The first spring I could walk through, I'm being posed among
The arbor and climbing vines, the hewn stone of the stair,
Looking back toward a camera that keeps shuttering the air,

Or off beyond it to a world grown suddenly out of reach—
The way the moments turn claustral, frame by frame.
Just outside the photos is the house in which my mother died,

And the house of my memory of her. The honeysuckle
On my grandmother's dress, which must have been my garden
And flowering bed, will be gone in another autumn, like her,

Though I don't remember either, or the yard in which
Whoever is taking these snapshots has thought to pose me.
Or why, in each, my eyes are so pale and wary and wide.

ON THE PHOTOGRAPHS IN MARGARET BYINGTON'S *HOMESTEAD: THE HOUSEHOLDS OF A MILL TOWN*

Russell Sage Foundation, 1910

I

After the frontispiece—its halftoned wards
And mill yards, the bridge's reflection
On the river like rain—the first photograph

Looks generic at first: two balloon-frame
Houses duplicated down to the vines
At the corner of each porch. Clapboard

And dormers, double-hung windows
Sashed in sets, the smoke-blighted trees
By the walks. Nearly new, their gray's

Already local like the weather, but no more
Familiar than that, until I read the caption:
Sixteenth Avenue. "Welcome home,"

It doesn't say, or, "Remember when?"
But then how could it? And whose memory,
Anyway, would be the one at work here

Early in the century? Not Byington's, nor
Lewis Hine's, who actually took the photo,
Nor mine, who haven't yet been born there.

II

This one's a different matter: the bandstand
Where we played fort in the park below
The library. Part pavilion, part breeze-filled

Porch, with its railing and little hipped roof.
"Frozen music," Goethe called architecture,
A form in which to reside. Here, you'll have

To imagine snatches of Sousa floating out
Above the Sunday crowds and, after that,
Our laughter, pitched like flutes in a wood.

III

The library itself, its turrets and cope-stoned
Chimneys, dusky brick—an Alexandria rising,
Even then, above the stacks and ashen town.

CHARTING THE LEAVES

That summer of rooftops and rain gusting in columns
Through the city—winged seeds darkening the maple,
      Seeds like sinters in the cigar tree—

I spent my mornings in the small room under the eaves,
My afternoons in Oakland, upstairs in the library.
      There in hushed rooms where evening

Seemed always about to fall, the slumbering jets
Of gas-lamps to flicker like wings and lift into the dusk
      Of the nineteenth century, I sat among

Actual ledgers of dust, now copied onto spools of film,
Discovering how the dead get lost as well in their own
      Bureaucracies, the faded lines of script

Grown ghostly as the hands that crabbed them. In aisles
Where the past is kept in stacks, I hunted through files
      For the names and dates I came from,

Finding my way among branches of a tree grown leafy
With births and deaths, the 1910 census with numbers
      For my mother's house of 3 children born,

2 remaining alive, the lines back to Glasgow where
My great-grandfather fled the same gray industrial slums
      He'd come to here in Homestead.

I searched through indexes and obituaries, found
Addresses on Amber Street and the drowned wards
    Of Johnstown, feeling my blood

Seine out. Ulster and Kilmarnock. And yet my mother's
Mother, where was she, with a quarter of my history
    And a name I'd been told meant *owl?*

Whatever source I leafed through, she was never there,
Nor the moon-faced bird illuminating my journey
    From the dark crown of its word.

PARK ELEMENTARY SCHOOL

I

Corpse, I said, and was corrected.
"It's pronounced *core,* Marine Corps."
Then someone else started to read.

Clouds of abrupt, smudged chalk
Filled the blackboard behind her.
The sprung shades were faded as leaves.

I'd have the same problem later
With *copse,* seeing the stark bones
Of birch trees inside the word.

And on the map—in the space above
The timber line where the world
Went blank—I could see lurking

All those Eskimo words for snow
I'd never have learned. Pages turned.
A white dust coated the chalk rail.

II

Among the slant drills and cossetings
Of Palmer Method, fractions
And the names of states, we stood

In lines for spelling bees, in crowds
Of those ousted at Musical Chairs.
History meant the Hessian Christmas

Followed by the Peace of Ghent.
Somehow the crack in the Liberty Bell
Was something good, and Justice

Looking like Blind Pew. We drew
The heart as a furnace, colored
The branching systems red and blue.

III

When you took green from the leaf
You got autumn. When you added up
Your family you got a tree.

Nine times nine was a number
That added up, magically, to nine.
I liked that. It meant *resolution*—

Though I didn't yet have the word—
Like dividing octaves on a piece of twine,
Or light into the colors of the spectrum.

WOOD FROG, FRICK PARK

Looping my way along the trail,
The underboughs swimming in light,

Green growing on the creek wall,
I come upon the frog: fist-sized,

Nearly mineral, a clump
Of so much Celsius and intelligence

As the earth requires. *Amphibian,*
I remember, tadpoles suddenly veering

Into another life. In ninth grade
And the throes of our own transformations

We sat around the long, gouged-
Out table, making the sign of the cross

In the chests of frogs, peeling back
Their shirtwaists to reveal

The numinous splay of organs
Like a well-packed drawer.

Breath was a kind of skin,
We learned, in which they came wrapped,

And how to make the dead limbs
Twitch, and how they pissed away

A fourth of their weight each day.
We lifted them from dripping vats

And ransacked their bodies,
Just the way we'd been taught.

In college, one biology professor
Had a frog he kept in his icebox:

The hibernating "pet" he'd show
To one group of students after another,

Bringing it out like a cold cut
Or some run-through

For the resurrection—as though
It were only a joke,

And not the totem he'd found
With which to imagine his life,

Alone and shut up there among us
In that quiet little town.

CLASS PHOTOS

Delighted to be dressed like this in bow tie
And vest, my son sits among his classmates
In the photos he's mounted on his walls.

I haven't the heart to tell him how soon
The names will start to absent those faces,
The grains themselves like pixels of dust

When he tries to call them back. Or that loss
Is the knowledge we're brought to after all.
Upstairs I manage to unpack the small gray

Snapshot of my sixth grade class, posed
In the formal rows of light into which we're
Squinting, and spot myself sitting there,

Next to a girl whose features lie hidden
Within a sudden gust of hair. And who's that
Over on the other end, staring at the ground?

Other than names from the neighborhood,
Few if any remain. Today, try as I might
To reclaim them, only Eddie Lelake's comes

Back from oblivion, and with it the shy,
Distant classmate I remember. That drab girl
In back quit school. Illness perhaps, or transfer,

I forget. Some of these faces I can't remember
Having even seen before, yet there we are,
Bunched together on the future's lawn:

The first class from Franklin Elementary,
Saplings flaring behind us, their thin bark
Scarred with our initials and clumsy hearts.

WOOD WORK

This is because otherwise I might forget
How it feels to have pulled down
A whole half of a tree, and then another,
Having the last good shock of sap-
Wood twist in my hands, the branches
Wrench loose from the sky. Because
I want to remember the way it slumped
To the ground, the two great boles
Like ruins of the world's oldest grove.
Once down, I went about dismantling it,
Pruning the smaller branches, ripping
Through the rotten trunk and hard tooth
Of the limbs. I put my back into it,
Hacked the orchard in the stump down
Beneath the surface, started stacking
The pieces together for curing in the sun.

Before depression hammered him
With the vanity of things, my father
Worked with wood, fitting his measured
Boards together, raising up the grain.
Whole weeks I'd say goodnight
To sounds of bandsaw and sander, drill-
Bits spiraling their grooves. I'd stand
At the top of the cellar steps, breathing
The incense of motors and freshly
Ripped planks, the dark grove of balsams

That rose from inside the spruce.
This year, my own tree split and corded,
I think how, come fall, first frosts
Burning off the lawns, I'll wake to stack
Kindling in the cold belly of the stove
That fills my house with such wood.

THE ART OF THE COMICS, CA. 1960

Barber Shop, Homestead Park

The shop would be empty when we entered.
He'd come from the backroom, it always
Seemed, as though he were being disturbed,

Annoyed even, at having to spend his day
Like this, reconfiguring our scraggly
Flattops and regular cuts, stooping to raise

The chair those notches till our toes barely
Touched the footrest and we sat head down,
Collared with tissue, snapped in squarely

Beneath the sheet. Then the scissoring sound
Above us, the feel of the stiff comb
Riffling its rows. You could feel his frown—

Concentration or the wish to be alone
And undisturbed once more—although he'd shave
Your neck if you asked him: fresh hot foam

Churned from the dispenser, the straight razor
Stropped across that tanned leather strap.
And then the gradually emergent nape

Stypticed and talcumed, a ritual passage
We thought marked us as grown. Which is why
We went there after all. That, and the stacks

Of comic books, old ones you couldn't find
Anywhere, *Gang Busters* and *Sub-Mariner,*
The lurid, gore-spattered covers of *Crime.*

Kitchen, 126 West Oliver Road

My father fixing dinner. The usual
Those Saturdays when my stepmother worked:
A giant can of Dinty Moore brand stew

Slopped into the saucepan beginning to perk,
Bread and butter on the table, glasses
Filled with milk. Even if it's early, it's dark,

The weekend now over by more than half.
Even with the two of us, it's like eating alone.
The light above the table seems to cast

The room somehow out beyond the window
Where it floats in a farther casement.
Beyond that, bare limbs the color of charcoal.

I'm trying to remember. Does he say grace
Or only that dinner's ready, wash your hands?
Did we say anything about our days?

I'm trying to remember. There were bands
Of gristle in the meat, the butter was hard
To spread, Saturdays meant paper napkins.

On this one I've brought a comic to read,
Bright companion to pass the time: *Sergeant Rock
Of Easy Company,* or the *Justice League,*

When startled by sudden weeping I look
Up—"What's the matter, aren't I good enough
For you?"—from the pages of the book.

AT KENNYWOOD PARK

The summer my father tried to kill himself
By gobbling up all his pills at once,
My cousins brought me with them to the park.

There I had candy spun from the air,
Noah's Ark, the ratchety sound of coasters
Catching their gears above sheer and sudden falls.

We made our way down wide arcades
To ride great wheels into the sky, The Wave
Out above the dinning crowds below us

And paddle boats drifting on a lake of fire.
Later, the skirt of the merry-go-round furling
Like the lip of the surf, I hung on to the horse

Plunging stiffly beneath me—its teeth bared
By the bridle—eager for another orbit
And the furious music crashing about my ears.

Who wouldn't have wanted the world that way,
Where the only terror was laughter,
The haunted house you ran from wasn't your own?

HETTIE

Marcelled and middle-aged already by 1939,
    She stares back at you from the yard of the house
        You remember visiting less and less,
    Her dress printed with sprays of hydrangea—
Dust-colored blossoms like the blown ones
    Behind her which have not yet started to fray.
        I can almost smell her powder, the scented
    Tissues from her purse. She was my father's
Widowed sister, the aunt whose teeth clicked
    When she spoke, who lived alone above
        The couple she rented to, passing through
    Their rhythms as if they were part of her own.
I slept there once or twice, up the steep
    Shelved staircase in the attic keep, shipped off
        During another crisis at home. She fed me
    Brown slices of bread, fish that came glistening
From tins. Workdays, while she sat before
    The pulsing black hive of her switchboard
        At U.S. Steel, I'd take down trinkets
    From their stand, though the only toy among them
Was the palsy-headed dog whose nose tracked
    Magnets like a scent. I'd roam through rooms,
        Poking around in closets and drawers,
    Her vanity's fussy clutter. Or stretched out on
The couch, bored by the interminable soaps,
    I'd look up into the dark red ceiling she sat below,
        Alone each night, waiting for the angels

To break open each of their seven seals.
I'd stand in her living room before the spot-lit print
In which Jesus in white robes knocked
At the door, the portrait in her bedroom
Of the thorn-crowned head whose eyes
Would flutter open, their sockets drowned in blood.

III:
A Strike Packet

AT THE STEELWORKERS' MONUMENT DURING THE 100TH ANNIVERSARY OF THE HOMESTEAD STRIKE OF 1892

I

Across from the castings
On Eighth and West, I stop
Before the granite shaft
And read the crisp, blocked

Inscription honoring
The workers who were slain
In Homestead by hirelings,
A century ago. Once again,

I stare at that puddler
Incised before the furnace
Door, his slender rabble
Slanting into the fire,

The corona spilling over
Like a ladle, teeming
The tapped steel into molds.

II

In the glyphs facing the stele
I can trace in stone
The vanished passage of steel:
How the ingots were soaked

In their heating pits,
Then rolled into shapes
In a slabbing mill, fitted
And finished off as plate—

And how on the landing
Before the open oven doors,
I swept the slabs clean
Of scale with an ordinary

Broom, hard by those flames
From which the world I knew
Was cast molten into place.

ALEXANDER BERKMAN ADDRESSING MAY FIRST RALLY, UNION SQUARE, NEW YORK, 1908

Two years out of prison, "the man who shot Frick"
     Stands on the balcony of a shelter
  As though upon the platform of a train,
Right hand held above the railing,
       The high dome of his forehead centered
     In the photograph and solid with light.

Around him, immigrant and solemn, other faces
       Stare into that host which spills toward us,
  Out of history, from the foreground's
Crowded rows. Arrayed in bowlers, coats and ties,
       They might be attending a funeral
     Instead of fighting for one—

The lying-in-state of the state itself—
       Neither God nor Master. Looking back
  Across that grim and disastrous century,
I think of what awaits them
       Who have gathered there together,
     Fierce and hopeful as the spring:

Ludlow and Kronstadt, the rictus of prisons
       In which Debs and the Wobblies were locked,
  Dreaming of One Big Union. Yes, yes, I know,
The perfectibility of man's an outworn joke

No one can possibly believe. And yet
They still persist, grouped together

In the photograph as part of a formal tension,
        The way that old box camera has been set
Just left of symmetry, the dark shapes
Massing upward into a roof which,
        Wide as wings, spreads above Berkman
Who leans forward to speak.

TOURING CLAYTON, THE ESTATE OF THE INDUSTRIALIST HENRY CLAY FRICK

"Mr. Frick wanted everything
Updated and 'state-of-the-art.'"

Her white gloves direct us past
A screened-off fireplace, already

Out of date in 1892, the year
These tapestry-weight draperies

Were hung, the thrummed braids
Were fashioned for the finials.

I imagine the bustle of craftsmen
Stenciling walls or leafing

Thin sheaves of foil in place,
Sizing the flocked Victorian fabrics

Stitched with tinsel and mother-
Of-pearl there above the mantle.

Leery of servants, she tells us,
The Fricks locked their house-

Hold china in a closet each night,
Carried the silverware to its vault

Past these four tinted Graces
At the turn of the stair, webbed

In their leaded glass. In 1892,
She does not say, Frick walled

The millyard in Homestead,
Trying to lock the workers out.

Admiring handmade vases and damask,
It is impossible not to think

About Pinkertons in rented attack,
Strikebreakers and State Militia.

She mentions the attempted murder
Without noting Berkman's name

Or the politics of his anguish,
And passes on to the paintings

Frick suffered to the sulphurs
Of the Pittsburgh air. I think

Of the black vanished furnaces
Splashing fire, slag like hills

Of lava, my grandfather in 1905
Falling to his death in the mills.

"The faces of the children's dolls
Were all hand-painted,"

She is saying, "their little wigs
Fashioned with actual hair."

BERKMAN IN PRISON: WOODS RUN, 1900

In the History Center: Berkman's reputed dagger
Boxed in Plexiglas on the wall. A wooden toy,
Blade X'ed like a pie crust, too blunt to cut much

But butter, you'd think, or the ground beneath
Sterling Street to Western Penitentiary. Actually,
They used picks and shovels, a homemade drill—

The quartet who set up house across the street
In order to tunnel their 300 feet, and come up
In the prison yard just within the high east wall.

A plan jinxed from the start, they inched past
Gas mines and sewer leaks, the rocky substratum
Of the watershed. Three months they spent at it,

Breathing through a leather bellows, revising
The intricate drawings Berkman had smuggled out.
They're earning every penny Emma Goldman's

Been able to raise, though money's not the issue
Down there, or above them in the window either
Where Goldie Kinsella sits all day at that piano,

Covering the bass of their digging with filigrees
Of popular song. Foster, this being Pittsburgh,
And Philip Sousa for the guards across the way,

Parading on their wall. And best of all, for herself,
Scott Joplin's "Maple Leaf Rag" echoing
Like a sulky at its slow stately pace, as though

The hours were idle as sunlight falling on the stones.
Taking time from his *Prison Memoirs*, Sasha
Writes, "I'll make the break, though there's not

one chance in a hundred for success." He's right.
Before he can even try, on the fifth of July,
Eight years from the eve of Homestead, a pile

Of bricks gets unloaded which blocks off the hole
Discovered weeks later by someone in charge.
Whistles and lockdown. Body count. Though it's not

A guard who's sent back down the tunnel
But a sewer worker who finds the abandoned house,
The few sheets of music left behind.

THE BANDSTAND

for John Gibb

A mitered, light-filled carpentry,
It stood alone on the green below the library,

Newels and posts and balustrades,
A roost in which we'd rest from our games.

I didn't know it then, but back in 1888,
During the Age of Parasols, my great-

Grandfather conducted the Carnegie Band
There on Centennial Day. Music stands,

Mill workers like jockeys decked in silks,
Their brass horns flashing: all the racetrack,

Cloud-topped feel of a Sunday in the park,
Worlds away from collective bargaining.

And yet in his letter to the *Local News*
He's breaking down the lump sum the union

Paid his musicians—$3.50 per man—
And raging about the rival Excelsior Band

Who sought to undermine them, driving
Wages down. "We are very much laboring

under the impression that such an act
unmasks the black-sheep, scab or rat,

as the case may be." Sounder economics
Than that gospel-of-wealth nonsense

Carnegie liked to spout. Four years later
Such squabbles will appear even quainter.

Halfway up the hillside, during the strike,
Militia will be tented at the concert site.

Bugles at sunset. The sounds of the gun.
To which the crystal is lifted at Clayton.

THE HOMESTEAD LOCKOUT & STRIKE, 1892

*. . . the lockout in Homestead had become the most
famous industrial conflict in American history, an
"honor" it arguably retains to this day . . .*
—Paul Krause, *The Battle For Homestead, 1890–1892*

I.

"Fort Frick," the workers called it, meaning
The fence and towers he'd ordered built about
The mills, barbed wire tautened from a looping
Script in which the knowing could read lockout,
Scabs, cold stoves in the dead of winter,
A non-union shop. When it came, Homestead
Had sentries set all along the river
And roads into town, a steamboat, the *Edna*,
Patrolling the waters, pickets posted
On the bridges as far off as Pittsburgh
Where one night they spied barges being towed,
A flotsam of Pinkertons on the current.
The alert was sounded. By four A.M.
The millgrounds were crowded with waiting men.

2.
for my grandfather, Robert Gibb

Like the rest of Homestead he'd lain awake
Those nights, listening now for nearly a week
To something like the last dissolving wake
Of sound, barely audible, as it leaked
From the locked mills. Silence filled his room.
Out the window, in the absence of smoke

And surgent clouds of soot from the flues,
He could see the stars, burning and remote,
The color, almost, of coal fires. And then
It came to him that what he'd been hearing
All that time were the gas flames flaring
From the street lamps—small blue jets
It seemed were everywhere out there,
Roaring above the dark wards of the river.

3.

The gangplank having flung down its gauntlet,
Men were struck by gunfire before cover
Could be found, among them George Rutter,
Gut-shot, wounded in the thigh. Bullets
Sizzled like magnesium into the river.
They dinged off the barges, off the scrap steel
And pig iron piled before the mills—
Positions that were held till it was over,
Workers launching their futile cache of rockets
From the Fourth, and Roman candles,
While Joseph Sotak was being bundled
Off to the hospital to bleed to death
And reinforcements arrived with dynamite,
The musty cannons they couldn't sight.

4.

Thomas Weldon died instantly. John Morris,
Forehead shattered, let out a shout
Before tumbling from the pump house
Into the wet earth trenched before it.

I number him as well. And Henry Striegel, slain
Near the wharf from which they'd sought
To torch the barges. Peter Fares and Silas Wain.
"You cannot take this from our mouths,"
Fares said dying, clutching a loaf of bread. The raft
They sent blazing toward the Pinkertons
Drifted away, the freight car jumped its tracks.
Each new failure drove them on, for over eleven
Hours, barricaded in the smoke and gore,
South of the river, on the colder shore.

5.

In Dabbs's photograph, following the battle,
The barges have been finally set on fire—
A victory more pyrrhic than actual,
Dark clouds billowing over the mill shore
In a great plied mass, spilling upward
Out of the picture, above the watery horizon
Which splits the work in half: the murky
Buildings divided from their reflections,
The smoke churning upward from its cindery
Twin burning head down in the stream.
It's either evening or nineteenth century,
That light's dissolve into longshot and time,
The world over water, its ashen stacks,
Guttering on the surface like a match.

6.

When he burst into Frick's office, dazzled
For a moment by the moted light streaming

Into the room, he seemed adolescent
As a lover, which he was: history's darling
On his first big date, trembling with a passion
That brought Frick to his feet, though too late
To do anything but flinch as the gun
Went off and bullets penetrated
His neck twice before they knocked Berkman down.
Even then, ardor undiminished,
He managed to crawl toward the sound
Of the wounded Frick and try to finish
Him off with a dagger. Then one last gasp:
The fulminate of mercury he almost gnashed.

7.

The day a young Guardsman named Iams shouted
"Three cheers for the man who shot Frick,"
And meant it, the words were barely out
Before he was arrested for sedition
And sentenced to be strung up by his thumbs
Until the taut bones slipped their sockets
And he hung—a slack, broken, pendulum
Turning on the tips of his toes. Unconscious
When they cut him down, he woke on Sunday
To be sheared and shorn of his uniform,
Drummed out of a regiment that was paid
To help break the strike. Coercion's the norm,
The town and mill grounds now under wraps,
The militia ensconced in its bivouac.

8.

By the first snows of winter it was lost,
Homestead, my Catalonia: eighteen-
Hundred strikers left unemployed, their jobs
Gone to scabs, the municipality
Taken over by industry shills.
Within a year it would be another
Squalid company town—numbing labor,
Wages down, private cops prowling the mills.
"Life worth living again," wired Carnegie
From Europe, dedicating monuments
As always to his own munificence,
And dreaming of the Homestead Library:
Turreted, vast, imposing. "An emblem,"
He liked to claim, "of harmony and union."

195 FATALITIES IN STEEL PLANTS OF THE PITTSBURGH DISTRICT, JULY 1, 1906–JUNE 30, 1907.—BY CAUSES

Cause	*Number of Fatalities*
Hot metal explosions	22
Asphyxiation by furnace gas	5
Operation of rolls	10
Total	37 (19 percent)
Operation of broad gauge railroad . .	18
" " narrow gauge railroad	13
" " cranes	42
Total	73 (37 percent)
Falling from height or into pit	24
Electric shock	7
Loading and piling of steel and	
iron products	8
	39 (20 percent)
Due to miscellaneous causes	46 (24 percent)
Total number killed in	
steel making	195

{ 57%

LEWIS HINE IN HOMESTEAD

Camera slung before him like an accordion,
He's haunting the wards of Homestead,
The courts and tenement yards, a peddler
Hawking his own flames and sparks,
The flash of powder above him in the pan.

"Light is required," he's insisted, "in floods."
He'll need it here, where mill smoke
Darkens the panes of glass through which
The world gets seen. *The Wounds of Work,*
For instance, or *An Arm Gone at Twenty.*

Or this *Man on Crutches,* the stump
Of his leg extended as if he were stepping
From the curb. A kind of tripod,
He's balanced there on the sidewalk,
More suspended, it seems, than posed:

One more pause in the hours, undivided
By shifts, among which he's been cut loose.
Bowler hat and moustache. The suit coat
Bunched up under his arms. And whether
It's resignation or the particulate air,

His eyes now are closed—unlike Hine's,
Who's squinting above the viewfinder,
Busy with the slide. Studying the photo,

I recognize the lapped style of clapboard
Siding the house he's used for a backdrop,

Its shutters and wood-planked stoop.
And that pant leg empty as a coal chute?
Half a century later, we learned about
Such mishaps on the labor gang, where
I passed among the lists of the maimed.

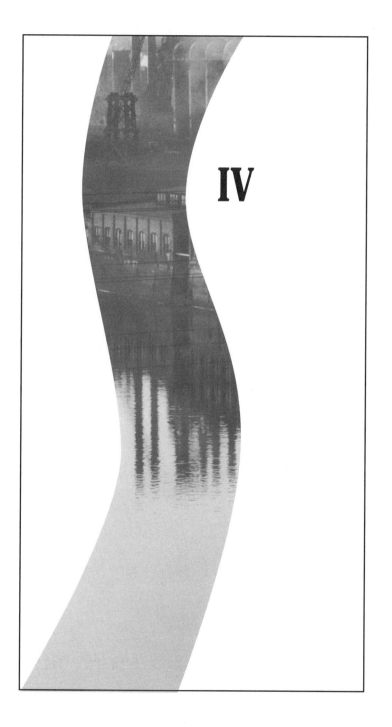

IV

MELVILLE VIEWS THE HOMESTEAD WORKS

A beached fleet of whale ships! As if
The manufactory had somehow come
To rest, here among the inland hills
And foundry of the rivers, mill fires
Smoky as try-pots rendering their fats.

He's already watched the iron mouths
Of furnaces being stoked, nights before
The mast when they pulled the fire-board
Back, but not a whole armada torched
At once, an open field for a brick-kiln.

And not, like this, in endless shifts—
A hoist for a windlass, blow stacks, gouts
From the soot-filled flues. Avoid staring
For long into the face of the flames,
He'd cautioned, but here there's little else.

Maybe, as he's beginning to think,
All hammered steel is woe? At least
For those who make it. And maybe
All manner of making ends in steel?
Eighteen thousand men manned the industry

He'd shipped in, casking oil for machinery
And lamps, fueling the dream
Of *plain mechanic power* he'd despaired of

During the war. *Rivets and iron-clads,*
the ringing of plate on plates . . .

He's thinking it's Empire that's being
Tried out there, grim navies
Of steelworkers in the yards of the mills.
Notes the pulpit above the ladles,
Steel hissing in the sulphur of the whale.

MESTA WORKER AND GEAR, 1913

Uncredited Photograph,
American, Twentieth Century

Sprocket and circumference, coin of the realm . . .

Even in the photograph it would cog a good-sized clock.
On the shop floor it stands on end, chocked by beams,
Clear to the banks of windows running beneath the roof,

The worker beside it posed, it would seem, for no reason
Other than scale, as with photos of sequoias, drawings
Of the great whales. The tread alone comes up to his shins—

Overalled and awkward, Lilliputian—the I-beamed spokes
Like massive Roman fives. Buttressed by bolts where
The driveshaft goes, the hub itself sits half a figure high.

They thought of the heavens like that: notched wheels
Milled to precision, worked twelve-hour shifts in the forge
Of metals being cast, each half axis of the fallen world.

GALLERY GUIDE

LIGHT!
The Industrial Age: 1750–1900
Art and Science, Technology and Society
                    —Carnegie Museum of Art

1. Orrery with Tellurian and Lunarium, ca. 1765

It looks like the workings from inside a watch,
The cogs and gears and start-up orbits,
Or music box on top of which the frozen figures waltz.

The universe as ingenious machine!
Reciprocal and dainty, each perfectly turned bearing
Circling in place as if keeping time.

As if God were an English eccentric
Tinkering with this latest toy, the classical mechanics,
Tapping the planets into alignment.

2. Glass of Water and Coffeepot, ca. 1760

And Chardin, having prepared a table
Before us, lucent and spirit and calm.

How artfully he's grouped his surfaces
On the still life's little shelf

And lit them, delighting in the exactitudes
By which they take place—glass

And ceramic, the clustered knobs of garlic
Opaque within their papery skins—

That gradient of green wall behind it all,
Part backdrop, part altar cloth.

3. *Camera Lucida, ca. 1750*

Elegant as pairs of calipers, lenses
Mounted in sets atop each stalk,
They might be something from a kit,
Or reading lamps whose cones of light
Fell cool and sheltered from jewels.

Artists used them, tracing the shapes
That refracted onto their pages,
Intuiting the rules of perspective—
How sight converged down corridors
Along which objects were fixed.

I thought they looked like periscopes
In the ads inside my comic books,
Alongside those for "chronographs"
And "satellite flash-lites,"
The ways of the world still magic.

4. *Lacemaker's Globe, ca. 1800–1850*

A lit, transparent pearl, stoppered on top,
The globe filled with water, the water
A lens in which light is held, candle power
Magnified and focused like attention

In the flame-sized caustic where threads
Were tied and what's incremental widened—
As if lace were an intricate physics
Whose fabric wove the whole of space.

5. *Camera, ca. 1850–1875*

Bulky as a toy-chest, with its locomotive's
Lamp and unclamped, accordion bellows,
The winched tracks along which it's slid.
Wood, brass, and canvas: an apparatus
For the conveying of light. Even the negatives
Hung in place like upright sheets of water
Are firmly boxed, and the base below them
With its crankshaft and handle and drop-
Forged parts. The three legs bent from the oak.
And those Victorians posed before it,
Eminent and upside down where the mist
Of their likeness passes into the glass.

TRAPPER BOY, COAL MINE

Photograph by Hine

Whatever the ruse, Hine has managed
To haul his cumbersome, essential tools
Down here to photograph this trapper boy,
Seated in darkness, hundreds of feet

Underground. He must be twelve or so,
Old enough to have survived the breakers—
Those long, tumbling chutes of coal
From which boys snatched shards of slate.

Now his only job is to listen all day long
For coal cars rattling their tracks
And open that door beside him and shut it
Fast, before a down-draft chills the shaft.

Ten hours at a time! No wonder the door
Has been livened like the caves at Lascaux:
The speckled, lyre-shaped birds he's drawn
Descending upon whatever winged insect

Or seed he's pictured beneath their beaks.
Perhaps it's Pentecost he's imagined
In that flame-traced flocking, the lamp
On his cap throwing shadows off the walls?

Think of him there, face against the door,
The breath at his mouth like a bird,
For thou wilt not leave my soul in hell,
Feeding him on this vision of the word.

PITTSBURGHESQUE, CA. 1949

Photograph by Selden I. Davis

A train from out of a tunnel, plumed and monumental,
The engines' soundless pulsing like a pressure
In your bones. Metal in a soot of shadow,

Light siphoning upward into a dim flat haze,
As though the city were zones of atmosphere,
Stone avenues receding in sheets of rain—

The mists from which the train comes looming,
And the dark vault of Union Station that arcs into
The foreground. It's all very postwar and noirish,

This mineral gray RKO sfumato, men in snapbrims,
The parked cars gleaming and sleek. 1949.
My father remarried, that long black train coming on.

SMOKESTACK LIGHTNING

In the newsreels it's funereal even during the day,
    A landscape topped with flues, smoke
        Like tethered plumes above the sulphur haze

From the ovens. Swing shifts you'd see it
    Two turns out of three. Then the night sky blazing
        Above the chimneys, *smokestack lightning*

shining just like gold. Driving to work and back
    You'd see the sign: "These Mills Have Now
        Operated Safely ___ Days Without an Accident,"

That slot like a lottery, its grim impending sum.
    We followed the countdown while the numbers
        Piled up. *What's the matter here?* Howlin' Wolf

Growling from 1956, the band locked
    In its steady groove, a slow freight on the tracks.
        Every schoolboy knew the answer to that.

What he didn't know he learned later, firsthand
    On the job, cautionary tales of men struck
        By cranes or crushed beneath machinery,

never see you no more, men lost in molten steel.
    The first version I heard was the Yardbirds',
        Live in some subterranean club, sound fraying,

Shearing out, as though someone were running
    A shaver down the Stratocaster's strings,
        Jamming the towering amps with feedback.

When I heard links of the wrong chain snap
    Above me, I was lucky the stacked slabs caught,
        What's the matter here? since it was days before

We learned about the differences in gauge.
    Whole weeks passed before we learned what not
        To have done, clearing the sharp strips from

The shears—spur-edged slivers caught in paste—
    Or which notes mattered in that maze of clatter,
        Crossing the switching yard. Brake-locks

And whistles, *stop your train,* the bent reeds
    Of the harp. I couldn't get out of there too soon.
        But first I'd have to hear how in the hours

Before us, *tell me baby,* back in that privy
    Taking a piss, someone tried to trip the window shut
        And wound up slamming through the bones

Of his hand. Some blues there's just no quitting,
    Don't you hear me calling, calling you?
        Maimed because a cold rain was blowing in.

FINGERED

All winter I worked in the cellar
Of the silversmith shop, polishing
Baubles, grinding seams
From name bracelets and rings.

What light there was seeped
From the lone window above us
Where the exhaust fan snuffled in air
Laden with silver dust and pumice,

The burning oils of the machines.
We stood there for hours, pulling
Hoops against the whirring rods
Till they were buffed as cutlery,

The jewelry grown so hot we had
To hold it with paper towels.
I hauled up trayfuls all day
To be displayed in gleaming cases,

Paused on my way back down
To hawk the gritty spittle
From my throat, wishing once more
For another day cast from the same

Gray mold to be finally over.
I was probably polishing that same

Wish when the bracelet pinged
Across the room and a voice cried

Out that he'd just lost the top
Of his finger, holding his hand
So we might see the nick of light
Above the first knuckle, and then

The blood, as though artesian,
Welling up. Sifting through
The sludge of filings in his tray
We found it, almost drained

Of color, and hurried it with him
To the hospital, where they tried
To graft it back. Before the week
Was over, it had already started

To tarnish—a fingertip made of
Putty which stiffened as it dried.
The year before, in the mills,
We learned to expect such things,

Hearing them inventory injuries
At the start of each shift, but
It was the next job, at the deli,
That I sliced off the barest

Sliver of finger, a wafer so thin
It vanished among the other meats
I was draping into their trays.
And by that time I'd seen enough.

INDUSTRIAL RELICS, STATION SQUARE

1. Brick Press and Electric Furnace

Here, as if set in threes on cooling racks,
Are the hard, rectangular loaves I remember
Lining the furnace walls, bisque-colored
And featherweight, the balsa of the bricks.

We'd come upon them in waiting stacks—
Gold for the straw of the fire. Or collapsed
In ovens and soaking pits where we'd be sent,
The slabs backing up, and the ingots.

2. Bessemer Converter

And up there, above the court, the great
Black egg-shaped barrel hovers on its axle,
Pitted with rust, the slobber of metal
On the vessel nose crusted like barnacles

Or callus on a right whale's head. Welds
And bolts. And because nothing should be lost,
The adz-shaped toggles where the wind box
Was clamped in place, the firestorm caught.

3. Blowing Engine, Shenango Furnace Co.

A pair of wheels mammoth as a grist mill's
Functions as the base for the piston

Balanced above them like a water tank, steel
Painted lime against the weather. Switched on,

It once drove gusts from banks of stoves set four
To the furnace, winds hot enough to melt
Down pipe, iron ore churning in the molten core,
The shriek and bedlam of the smelters.

4. *Benches, Bessemer Courtyard*

That sun-dazzle out on the river, as if
A shoal of luminous fish were roiling the surface
Near the Smithfield Street Bridge.
Beyond it the ramps on which traffic's ridged,
In-bounds and out, the wall of the city
Like glass vaults sheared from the sky.
At the end of summer, mid-afternoon, light glints
Halfway down their sides: particles of wind
The cameras catch for us, time-lapsed,
On the news—the steady-state of shoppers,
Clouds leveling in above the wharf.
Behind me the last tourists pose, dwarfed
By the relics, then drift off toward the parking lots.
Light on the water webs the bridge's blocks.

KHRUSHCHEV VISITS MESTA MACHINE, 1959: A VARIATION ON THE DOUBLE SONNET

The mills are down. No floodlit cumulus
Spilling out. No hard freight switched in the yards.
Because of the strike, he'll be ushered up
To Mesta instead. Limos and bodyguards,
Crowds lining the street. It's late September
And the Cold War, stockpiles of coke and steel
Mounded along the river like those he remembers
Growing up in the Ukraine. Still reeling
From the treatment given him so far—
Insults flung from dais and press—he's touched
To have such a turnout, and is hardly
Out of the car when he's greeted in Russian,
That gilt-domed tongue, by an excited janitor
From Minsk. Before long, in their shop-floor

Form of détente, he's happily working
The crowd, introducing a glum Gromyko
When a clerk named Jackey, ignoring
The guards, gives Khrushchev one of his own
Cigars. In return he's handed the wristwatch
Which he raises into the air, silver
Flashing, the clamped band soviet and squat.
That evening in the *Daily Messenger*
We'll see it below his own, there on the wrist
He's held out, laughing, for the photo.

Only two years from the panic of Sputnik
There's no way that any of us could know—
One watch for time, the other for history—
How soon it would all be gone, come victory.

DREAM STREET: W. EUGENE SMITH'S PITTSBURGH PHOTOGRAPHS

They hold the shapes of our light
In surfaces of silver—halides and gelatins—
Contact like the laying on of hands
Or the fossil leaf printed on the sidewalk,

As though light were a falling body
Here come to rest, the circumference
Of darkness around it. In the darkroom
At four A.M., "Blue Monk" bright on the hi-fi,

He's at work, at home, cropping shots,
Deepening the contrasts of light and shade:
The platinum of the train tracks,
Barges seen like dark drowned wings

Being freighted down the river,
The blast-furnace sun having back-lit the hills,
That tugboat the size of a shanty
Perched above the deep rungs of its wake.

Man carries his loneliness with him,
A blown-up letter reads, *regardless of place.*
In the title photograph, the street sign
DREAM marks place the way it seems

In sleep—this world focused through
Another, both familiar and strange.
Here, years later, where every image
Quickens the surface of time, I dream

Of being home. "He sounds just like you,"
My wife says, reading the wall-sized text,
Crowds of tourists wandering past us
Guided by cassettes, crowds from the city

Of my childhood covering the walls:
Commuters under umbrellas, shoppers
At street-level tiered beneath the beams
Of another building being hurried up.

Smokestacks and steeples, the stark copse
Of chimneys like soot-stained trees.
It has no business being beautiful,
Any of it, not the bridges on their old

Stone stanchions or the sheen of the rivers
Strewn with fire. Geysers of steam
Erupting as if from fissures in the earth.
The planet's worth of clouds. At night,

Crossing over, we passed between flames,
The armadas of the mill yards burning,
Or days the skies were mirror
And flawless as polished steel.

NOTES

"Deed": The Homestead martyrs are the seven striking steel-workers killed by Pinkertons on July 6, 1892.

"Raising the Blinds": The description of the street scene in section one alludes to details in Alfred Stieglitz's photograph, *From My Window*.

"The Hall of Architecture": The terms "freight and plunder" were first configured by James D. Van Trump in *An American Palace of Culture, The Carnegie Institute and Carnegie Library of Pittsburgh* (Carnegie Institute, 1970).

"At the Steelworkers' Monument during the 100th Anniversary of the Homestead Strike of 1892": A "puddler" was a skilled ironworker, a "rabble" a rod with which molten iron was worked.

"Alexander Berkman Addressing May First Rally, Union Square, 1908": The poem takes its title, and physical details, from an uncredited photograph (University of California, Riverside). *"Neither God nor Master"* is an old Anarchist maxim.

"The Homestead Lockout & Strike, 1892": The conflict began as a lockout, Frick and Carnegie seeking to break the union. Frick hired Pinkertons to seize the mills but they were repulsed on July 6, in what became known as the "Battle of Homestead." The town was subsequently taken over by State Militia and placed under martial law. Alexander Berkman, a strike sympathizer and lover of Emma Goldman, came to Pittsburgh and on July 23 tried unsuccessfully to assassinate Frick. Carnegie, through it all, was fishing in Scotland.

"195 Fatalities In Steel Plants of the Homestead District, July 1, 1906—June 30, 1907.—by Causes": This list can be found in John A. Fitch's *The Steel Workers* (1911), one of six books published by the Russell Sage Foundation in its *Pittsburgh Survey*.

"Melville Views the Homestead Works": The italicized material comes from Melville's Civil War poem, "A Utilitarian View of the Monitor's Fight."

"Pittsburghesque. Ca. 1949": "Sfumato. In painting or draw-
ing, delicate fusion of tones from light to shadow." *A Writer's
Companion*, Louis B. Rubin, Jr., ed. (Baton Rouge: Louisiana
State University Press, 1995).

"Smokestack Lightning": The Howlin' Wolf version, quoted
throughout the poem, can be found most recently on *Howlin'
Wolf: His Best*, released by MCA/Chess in 1997. The phrase
"differences in gauge" refers to the width (and hence strength)
of the chain links.

"Khrushchev Visits Mesta Machine, 1959: A Variation on the
Double Sonnet": The irony, of course, is that "victory" in the
Cold War came at the expense of the rank-and-files of the U.S.
and U.S.S.R. The elite sectors of both countries made out very
well.